D1453889

Dessert First

Reflections on Stewardship and the Spiritual Life

Steve Clapp

A LifeQuest Publication

Dessert First
Reflections on Stewardship and the Spiritual Life

Steve Clapp

For further information, contact: LifeQuest, 6404 S. Calhoun Street, Fort Wayne, Indiana 46807; DadofTia@aol.com; 260-744-6510.

The names and/or locations of some persons quoted in this book have been changed to protect their privacy. All the stories that are shared are true.

Biblical quotations, unless otherwise noted, are from the New Revised Standard Version of the Bible, copyrighted 1989 by the Division of Christian Education, National Council of Churches, and are used by permission.

Research results shared in this publication have been provided by Christian Community, Inc., a partner of LifeQuest.

ISBN 1-893270-20-3

Thanks for the contributions made to this resource by Kristen Leverton Helbert, Sara Sprunger Clapp, the staff of Evangel Press, and the congregation of Lincolnshire Church.

Manufactured in the United States of America

Contents

You shall eat your fill and bless the
LORD your God for the good land
that he has given you.

Deuteronomy 8:10

And God is able to provide you with
every blessing in abundance, so that
by always having enough of everything,
you may share abundantly in every
good work.

2 Corinthians 9:8

Introduction

I wrote this *Dessert First* devotional booklet because it seems to me that our approach to stewardship education in the church is sometimes too far removed from the development of the spiritual life–and not nearly as much fun as it should be. Like most of those reading this booklet, I was raised to eat the "nutritious" portion of a meal before having dessert. The conditioning worked well. I like fish and fruits and vegetables. And living in our calorie-conscious time, I often skip dessert entirely. Although I was always reasonably generous in my giving to the church, my motivation used to be based on obligation and doing my fair or proportionate part of paying for the church's program.

A church member named Lucille had a different attitude toward dessert and toward giving. The first devotion in this booklet shares her perspective. She ate dessert first, and she gave first to God. That seems to go against human wisdom. We feel like we should eat the nutritious food first and then consider a small portion of dessert if we still have room. We also tend to use our resources of money, time, and talent to meet our own needs first and then give to the church and other charitable causes from what we have left. In North America, similar attitudes affect the way that we treat the valuable environmental resources God has provided.

When we accurately perceive the incredible blessings that God has given us, our hearts overflow with gratitude. With Christ alive in our hearts, we embrace the blessings of life, including dessert. Our motivation for giving is rooted in gratitude and thanksgiving rather than in guilt and obligation.

Our lives are filled with blessings, but in the hurry and pressure of daily life, we sometimes fail to recognize that reality. There are also times of grief and difficulty in which the problems we face seem to outweigh the blessings we've received. Yet in all seasons of life, in both the good and the bad times, our Lord is seeking to bless us and guide us.

Taking care of our bodies is part of being faithful to God. I don't want readers of this booklet to eat so much dessert that they have health problems! But occasionally eating dessert first can be a way of being in touch with the joy of life–with the rich gifts that our generous God has given us.

Week One: First Things First

Day 1: Eat the Pie First!
Read Deuteronomy 8:10–18

A church member named Lucille shared with me two interesting perspectives on life:

1. Lucille believed in eating her pie or other dessert before the rest of the meal. She said: "When you get to being seventy-eight years old like I am, you fill up quickly. I always want to have dessert, so I just eat that first."

2. Lucille also believed in giving ten percent of her money to God through the church before she spent anything else. She said: "I don't have a lot of money, just social security and a small pension, so it's easy to spend it all and have nothing left for God. What I've discovered in life is that when I really put God first, I end up having enough for everything else I need. In fact, I'm able to save a little bit of money each month. I don't know how God works it out; but it's like putting Him first causes everything else to work better."

She was an energetic, enthusiastic person who thoroughly enjoyed life; and she lived with a clear set of values and priorities. She intended to make the most of life–and to her, that meant eating dessert first and giving to God first.

The Deuteronomy passage warns us of the danger of forgetting God when times are good. It's easy for us to take our blessings for granted and to forget that God is the source of all that we have. Over the years, I've found that Lucille was right about the necessity of giving to the church first. Doing that helps me think more clearly about the other financial decisions I make. I also think she was right about eating the pie first, and I've often followed that advice, too!

Prayer: God, we give you thanks for the many blessings you give us. Thank you for pie, for financial resources, for good friends, and for your love. Help us to put you first not only in our giving but in our other decisions as well. Amen.

Day 2: A Siamese Reminder
Read 1 John 4:7–12

I had been away from home for a week attending meetings and conducting workshops. I had an enormous pile of snail mail and e-mail accumulated at my desk, and I was behind on a writing deadline. Tia, my Siamese cat, was desperate for my attention and jumped on my desk several times. Each time, I gave her a few perfunctory pats on the head and then moved her to the floor.

I left the study for a few minutes. When I returned, I found that Tia had knocked my mail, my papers, and two of my books onto the floor. Although she wasn't able to budge it, she was pushing against the computer. The message was clear: leave those things alone and give attention to your cat. I picked her up, moved to a comfortable chair, and spent some time stroking her and letting her rub against me.

Our lives are often filled with pressure, and it's easy for us to forget what's most important. Our work does need to be accomplished, and deadlines should be honored. But for what are we really working? If we don't have time for those we love, including our pets, then our priorities need examination.

Time management authority Stephen Covey has written an excellent book called *First Things First*. His title offers good counsel not just for time management but for our lives as a whole. We need to decide what things are most important and truly put "first things first." That is the essence of Christian stewardship and of the spiritual life.

Prayer: Help us, Lord, to be clear about our priorities. Be with us as we strive to keep our commitments at work and the church without neglecting those we love. Help us put first things first, according to your grace. Amen.

Day 3: A Place of Sanctuary
Read Psalm 127:1–2

When I drive from my home to my church during the week to bring materials to the office or to attend meetings, I find it easy to be frustrated by the trip:

- Some people drive too slowly.
- Some people drive too recklessly.
- Some people needlessly cut off others.
- Traffic lights are often uncooperative with my schedule.
- When I'm behind schedule in the morning or afternoon, I almost always find myself trapped behind a school bus.

On days when I feel that frustration deeply, the sanctuary seems to call me as I walk by the doors. When I am wise, I follow that calling, walk into the quiet space, sit in a pew, look at the altar, and say a prayer for all the people who frustrated me on the road. When I leave, I feel renewed and refreshed.

Automobile accident rates are high precisely because we are so often in too big a hurry and too quickly let ourselves become frustrated with others. My wife's car was rear-ended, as she sat at a stoplight, by a woman who was having an upsetting conversation on a cell phone. Fortunately neither driver was injured, but the automobile damage was significant.

We need places of sanctuary and times of sanctuary to keep our perspective on life. George Buttrick, a seminary professor and theologian, often said, "God knows how much time you have. God doesn't ask you to do more than you have time to accomplish. When you are overwhelmed, it's because you have permitted yourself to be overwhelmed. Find a quiet place and pray about what God truly wants you to be doing."

Prayer: In the midst of busy lives, Lord, help us to find places of sanctuary and to open our hearts to Your presence. Help us to see other drivers as our brothers and sisters through You. Amen.

Day 4: The Rivers of Creation
Read Genesis 2:4–14

My wife and I made a recent trip to Rocky Mountain National Park in Colorado. Friends had promised us that we would get to see elk because we would be there during their "rut" or mating season. When I saw the volume of automobile traffic in the area, I decided that I would be thankful to see just one elk. Why would elk risk coming so close to cars and people? My low expectations were blown away when we saw 55 of these beautiful animals congregated in a meadow, near a stream. We saw mountains, lakes, rivers, and animals in the park that literally took our breath away.

That evening as we drove from the park back to our motel, we found the highway blocked by another group of elk, perhaps 40 at that location. All of us willingly stopped our cars and watched these magnificent animals with amazement. There was truly a sense of God's presence in that place.

I have often said that there was nothing wrong with my own home state of Indiana that couldn't be cured by a mountain and an ocean. Indiana, in fact, does have its own natural beauty. While we don't have elk, moose, or bears, we have squirrels, raccoons, and an incredible variety of birds.

Wherever we live, we need to view the natural world as a rich gift from a loving God. The rivers of creation are not for us alone. They are for all life on the planet and for future generations as well. When we take actions as individuals, companies, and nations which pollute and destroy those resources, we are endangering the future and failing to recognize the Lordship of the One who caused the rivers to flow.

Prayer: Help us to cherish the natural resources that You have given us and to be responsible stewards for the future. Teach us to value all the resources You have provided and to make decisions that protect those resources. Amen.

Day 5: Teaching Stewardship
Read Proverbs 22:6

My friend Bob says that he serves on the board and mission groups at our church in part because it is one of the best ways to teach his children to be good stewards of their time. When he kisses them good night early before going to a meeting, he explains that he is seeking to serve Christ by using his talents wisely, meaning that:

- He is not gone every night of the week.
- He is willing to make some sacrifices for his church, just as he does for his job, because the work is important.
- He explains "stewardship" to them so they understand that God is the source of our talents and our time.

The words *steward* and *stewardship* aren't part of our daily conversation. In biblical times, a steward was a person who had been given responsibility for resources which belonged to someone else. The steward carried out the wishes of the owner of the resources. God has made all of us stewards of material resources, our time, our talents, our relationships, and the natural world in which we have been placed. When we make decisions about those resources, we need to consider what God wants us to do with them rather than just what we want.

God in fact has invited us to be partners in the care of the world in which we have been placed. In John 15:15, Jesus explains the relationship He desires with us:

I do not call you servants any longer, because the servant does not know what the master is doing; but I have called you friends, because I have made known to you everything that I have heard from my Father.

Prayer: Help us, Lord, as we seek to have balance in our lives. Help us teach our children what it means to be good stewards of what we have been given. Help us to recognize our time, our talents, our material resources, our relationships with others, and the natural world as Your gifts to us. Amen.

Day 6: Worrying about Money
Read Matthew 6:25–34

Joy and her husband feel overwhelmed with debts from their college educations, a large mortgage, two car payments, and credit card bills. Joy visited with her grandmother and observed that her grandparents seemed to have gone through life without such anxiety.

Her grandmother laughed and said, "I can't think of many times when your grandfather and I didn't have at least some financial concerns. That was especially true since we owned the restaurant for so many years. Each time we had to take on a new debt for renovation or expansion, I'd feel like we were jeopardizing our future. But your grandfather would just say, 'Well, the worst that can happen is that we lose the restaurant and the house. Then we start over. But we aren't going to lose our love, our children, or each other. And God is always with us.'"

Eighty-nine percent of people in North American feel strong financial anxiety at least some times each year, and 54% feel that anxiety almost all of the time [Christian Community study]. Jesus seeks to set us free from that worry:

- We are set free from that worry when we recognize that God is with us no matter what happens and that what we truly need will always be provided.
- We are set free from that worry when we recognize that the accumulation of material possessions should not be the top priority in our lives. Different choices can lower the financial pressures on us.

Prayer: Help us, Lord, to keep perspective. May we put our trust in You and recognize that You are with us as we move into the future, whatever our financial circumstances. Help us make choices which will lower the financial pressures on us. Amen.

Day 7: Living More with Less
Read Matthew 6:19–21

I decided to count the number of advertisements shown in a commercial break of a popular television show. Ten advertisements came at me in the space of only a few minutes time. Among other things, I was offered:

* The opportunity to claim the respect to which I'm "entitled" by buying or leasing a luxury automobile.
* The opportunity to enhance my sex life by persuading my doctor to prescribe a medication.
* The opportunity to show how much I care about my children by shopping for them at a particular department store.
* The opportunity to have a great time with my family by taking them to a particular restaurant chain.
* The opportunity to prove my financial insight by changing my mortgage to a particular bank.

The truth is that I do not "need" anything that was offered in the advertisements. My personal worth most certainly does not rest in the kind of car I drive or where I choose to do my mortgage banking. I don't have to go shopping to prove that I care about my children, and it isn't necessary to go to a specific restaurant in order to have a good time with those I love.

Commercial advertising and our society teach us to measure our worth in terms of our professional success and our material possessions. We buy more expensive clothes, larger homes, and faster, bigger automobiles than we need. As a result, in an uncertain economy, many of us feel at risk for the future.

There is another way of living. It is possible for us to live more fully while we pull our personal expenditures back. God intends for us to enjoy life, but the things we purchase are not always sources of joy or fulfillment.

Prayer: Free us, Lord, from the temptation to measure our worth by our wealth and material possessions. Surround us with your love, and guide us in our decision-making. Amen.

Week Two: Money and Spirituality

Day 8: Honk If You Love Jesus
Read Deuteronomy 14:22–27

During the period of time in which the bumper sticker "Honk If You Love Jesus" was especially popular, one minister had a bumper sticker made which proclaimed:

> *IF YOU LOVE JESUS, TITHE!*
> *ANY FOOL CAN HONK!*

I don't think those bumper stickers had much circulation outside of the pastor's congregation, but the words do embody a truth that we easily miss: There is a direct relationship between our spiritual health and our stewardship of all the gifts our Lord has given us.

Talking about money is uncomfortable for many of us in the church. Sermons and classes on stewardship can easily feel intimidating; and words like *tithing, budget, guilt,* and *obligation* can make us want to be someplace else! Most pastors in fact do not like talking about money. In a survey of 1,450 clergy conducted by Christian Community, only 6% of the pastors felt comfortable preaching about financial stewardship.

Our Lord, however, had a lot to say about wealth and property. Matthew contains 109 references to the subject; Mark, 57; Luke, 94; and John, 88. Jesus spoke more about earthly possessions and stewardship than any other topic. The church as an institution did not exist during the earthly life of Christ, and His teachings weren't for the purpose of raising the annual budget for a congregation. Jesus spoke so much about wealth and property because our attitudes toward those material goods have so much to do with the spiritual life. Everything that we have comes to us by the grace of God, and our use of all our resources relates directly to our spiritual health.

Prayer: Help us, Lord, to truly recognize You as the source of all our material blessings. Teach us the spiritual significance of the financial decisions we make. Amen.

Day 9: A Christmas to Remember
Read Deuteronomy 31:6

A friend of mine shared this experience with me: *While facing the task of becoming a single Mom, I not only worried about being a good parent but also about adjusting to a new income. It was tough. It was at this time of my life that I learned to truly trust God, who gives us everything we need.*

Our first Christmas without the boys' father was the hardest. I felt lucky to pay my bills, let alone buy Christmas presents for my sons. I prayed and prayed that, because my boys had experienced such a rotten year, we could have a decent Christmas. The week before Christmas I was helping out in the church kitchen. I had placed my coat and purse on a table in the fellowship hall while in the kitchen. While driving home, I put my hand in my coat pocket and found a roll of money which totaled $100. I began to cry; it was very hard for me to accept the money because of my pride. In the past I had always received much joy in helping others, and now it was someone else's turn to help me.

When I arrived home, I checked the mail; and among the other letters, I found two unsigned Christmas cards containing $100 bills. One had the message: "Jesus wants you to have a good Christmas." The next day I found a cardboard box on my front porch. It was full of food items to use for Christmas dinner. Every day that week we received some type of surprise, in all over $500.

That Christmas was hard for me–letting down my pride and accepting gifts from others–but thanks to God and all his earthly angels, my boys and I had a wonderful Christmas. Since then I have had many more trials; but with each one I have grown in faith. When something does not go my way, I know it is because God has something special or better planned. My favorite verse, Deuteronomy 31:6, has always helped me through tough times: Be strong and courageous. Do not be afraid or terrified because of them, for the Lord your God goes with you; he will never leave you nor forsake you. *And the Lord has kept that promise.*

Prayer: Thank you, Lord, for keeping your promises to us, for meeting our needs in difficult times. Help us to be your messengers of kindness and generosity to others. Amen.

Day 10: A Forbidden Topic?
Read Matthew 6:24

In his book *Freedom of Simplicity*, Richard Foster points out that "personal finance is the new forbidden subject of modern society" [p. 138]. Pastors sense that view; and as shared in the devotion for Day 8, most of them are reluctant to talk about money in sermons or classes.

Yet Christian Community's research shows 75% of the members in the typical congregation would like to be doing more for the church financially! And when responding on an anonymous survey, 78% of the members said they would benefit from more opportunity to understand and discuss the spiritual significance of money in their lives and in society.

We sense the truth of Christ's warning in Matthew 6: that we cannot serve both God and wealth. We need opportunities to reflect on the place of money in our lives because of the deep spiritual significance of how we view and how we spend those resources.

If people want to be doing more for the church and for others financially than they are, why don't they do so? Contemporary life in North America brings strong economic pressure. Housing is expensive, cars are expensive, education is expensive, and medical care is expensive. Commercial advertising works hard to convince us that our worth is connected to our material possessions. Most Christians don't give more to the church because the other demands on their resources seem overwhelming. When we start to think seriously about what we actually need as opposed to what we want, our perspective can change. When we put first things first with our finances, everything else has a way of working out by God's grace.

Prayer: Lord, grant us a greater willingness to study the place of money in our lives. Help us to use our resources in ways that are pleasing to you. Amen.

Day 11: You Can't Afford Not To Read Deuteronomy 14:22

I know a couple who had a very difficult time financially during the first twenty years of their marriage. He was a pastor of two small congregations in a rural area, and the churches were often not able to fully meet payroll. In spite of that, the minister and his wife continued to give 10% of their small income back to the church.

I asked them why they had done that when the church failed to meet its obligation to them. They responded, "We always felt that we couldn't afford not to!" By putting Christ first, they discovered what many other people have–other financial needs work out. The more difficult the times, the more important it becomes to put first things first. When we recognize God as the source of everything, our lives are opened to blessings.

People who give generously to the church and to other charitable causes are not motivated primarily by guilt or obligation. In Christian Community's study on stewardship and the spiritual life, here are the top three reasons people shared for their giving to the church:

- Commitment to Christ.
- Desire to support the church's program.
- Belief that giving is a spiritual matter and that generous giving benefits one's spiritual life.

Two of the three top reasons are related to the spiritual life rather than to the program of the church. While almost everyone reading this booklet will be a person with deep commitment to the needs of the local church, it's important to remember that the most important reasons for giving relate to our own spiritual lives.

Prayer: Help us, Lord, in difficult times and in good times, to put you first in our financial decisions. Let our giving flow from the realization that You are the source of all things and from our desire to respond to You in gratitude. Amen.

Day 12: A Perfect Chocolate Soufflé
Read 2 Corinthians 9:8

A good friend and I shared a wonderful dinner at Chillingsworth's, a restaurant on Cape Cod. We had chocolate soufflé for dessert; and as we ate it, we talked about it being perhaps the best dessert we had ever had.

As we were finishing the meal, one of the owners came to us and apologized, saying that the chocolate soufflé was not supposed to have left the kitchen because it had not risen as high as their standards for serving. She was apologizing for what was one of the best desserts we had ever experienced. Talk about high standards! I share the story for two reasons:

First, there is a place for the good things in the Christian life. There is nothing wrong with a meal in a nice restaurant or with a fabulous dessert. Our Lord enjoyed sharing meals with people and changed water into wine for the wedding at Cana. The problem comes when the desire for the good things takes over our lives and becomes excessive. In our North American culture, many of us confuse *needs* and *wants*. Rather than seeing meals at good restaurants, nice clothing, comfortable cars, large homes, and exotic vacations as things we *want*, we become trapped into feeling that we *need* those things to feel good about ourselves.

Second, we honor God when we try to do our very best–whether making chocolate soufflé or working in the life of the church or taking care of children. Many of us work under constant time pressure, and there are times when it simply isn't possible to do our best work. When we have the opportunity to do our best, we should take it–making the most of the talents God has given us.

Prayer: We thank you, God, for being able to enjoy the wonderful opportunities in our world. Thank you for the good things of life which come to us from Your love. Help us to do our best with the talents You have given us. Amen.

Day 13: Anita as a Blessing?
Read Matthew 25:31–40

A woman named Anita has been coming to our church for financial assistance for ten years, interrupted by two short terms in jail. Anita is frustrating to help because she feels the need to tell a long story each time, and some of the stories are impossible to accept as fact–no one could have as many children in life-threatening circumstances as Anita claims! Yet she is clearly unemployable, falls through some of the cracks in the local social service system, and does need help.

I find it much easier to respond to the needs of Beth, who is a single parent struggling to raise three children after the death of her husband. She's employed full-time as a social worker and endeavors to help people like Anita as part of that job. The cost of care for Beth's youngest child, however, is so high that she has a very difficult time making ends meet on a social worker's salary. She occasionally needs some quiet help from our church's food pantry, and we are glad to supply it. She finds it difficult to accept the help because she is so accustomed to being the one who helps others.

Helping Beth is a pleasure; helping Anita sometimes feels like a strain. Yet there are many people like Anita who very much need our help.

Decisions about helping persons in need are often difficult, and those of us with comfortable lifestyles tend to be judgmental of those who are not doing as well economically. Our Lord, however, did not have a "worthiness" standard for responding to those with problems. The Gospel of Matthew reminds us that we encounter the living Christ in the poor and imprisoned of the world. The opportunity to help Anita reminds me of the blessings in my own life–so perhaps Anita is a blessing!

Prayer: Help us, Lord, to respond to the needs of others and to recognize your presence in those we help. Keep us from harsh judgments about those whose lives are more difficult than our own. Amen.

Day 14: Being Content
Read 1 Timothy 6:6–10

I have wonderful friends who have committed themselves to simple lifestyles. One couple are peace activists, who spend as much time as possible trying to persuade politicians and other leaders to make decisions that avoid the use of military force.

Some people consider this couple poor because of the simple lifestyle that they have chosen. In their case, however, their apparent poverty is not because they are unable to earn more money but because they have decided on different priorities for their lives. In addition to having a passion for peace, they also have a deep concern for those who are poor because of the circumstances of life rather than by choice. He takes cast-off bicycles and rebuilds them to provide transportation for the homeless and others who are poor. He also builds and sells solar ovens. The two of them maintain an impressive garden, and they freely share the produce of that garden with persons in need.

Their home is very plain; they don't worry about what they are wearing; and they do not care at all what kind of car they drive. Some people are made uncomfortable by the simplicity of their lives; others feel a need to "do more" for them to improve the quality of their lives. But they in fact don't want more than they have. They are very content with their standard of living and feel good about their accomplishments. They know a great deal about the contentment described in 1 Timothy, and the rest of us have much to learn from such people.

In a world that encourages living beyond our means and evaluating our self-worth by what we possess, the witness of people to a simple lifestyle is desperately needed.

Prayer: Help us, Lord, to find greater contentment in the simple things of life. Help us live with less anxiety and with fewer desires. Amen.

Week Three: Deepening Faith

Day 15: Transforming Lives
Read 1 Corinthians 12:14-31

People across North America were touched by the story of Cassie Bernall, one of the teenagers murdered at Columbine High School in Littleton, Colorado. She was shot immediately after saying "Yes" to a question about belief in God. Some view her as a contemporary martyr to the faith.

The best-selling book *She Said Yes*, written by Cassie's mother, talks about the reality that Cassie herself had been a very troubled teenager, in danger of going down a path very similar to that of the two young men who committed the horrible violence at Columbine. Her parents and a church youth group had a lot to do with her life being turned around. A close friend of hers describes what happened at a youth retreat:

> *I wasn't expecting much out of the whole thing, also not for her [Cassie], because she'd always been so closed. I thought: just one weekend is not going to change her, though it could help. So when she totally broke down, I was pretty shocked. . . Cassie was crying. She was pouring out her heart–I think she was praying–and asking God for forgiveness.*

The church is not just another institution. The church is the living, breathing body of Christ. And the church at its best transforms the lives of people of all ages. While the impact of a church in Colorado on Cassie Bernall gained especially wide recognition, the reality is that churches all across the country are continually changing the lives of people for the better. Worship services, youth programs, emergency assistance, and other congregational initiatives make a profound difference in the name of Christ. Those ministries are impossible without our prayers, our volunteer efforts, and our financial support.

Prayer: Lord, help me more fully contribute to the body of Christ through the work of my congregation. Guide me in praying on a regular basis, in volunteering my time and energy, and in giving generously of my financial resources. Amen.

Day 16: Partners With God
Read Mark 4:26-32

My wife shares this perspective on gardening and steward-ship: *My grandfather was a farmer. My grandmothers were Master Gardeners. My Aunt Carol is an expert on all living things–animals and plants! My mother, my cousins, and my sisters put me to shame where gardening is concerned. They've always been so interested and knowledgeable about the process! Oh, I've grown some flowers, herbs, and vegetables over the years; but I've done it more for the end result than the process (not always successfully, either!). Any successful results were more God's doing than mine.*

I can't explain it, but this year I've become fascinated, perhaps obsessed, by gardening thoughts–books and catalogs, perennials, bulbs, vines, even gardening tools! I think about growing delphiniums and hollyhocks. I'm expanding my flower bed–I envision a cottage garden in my back yard. Could it be that my "gardening gene" (I must have one!) is moving from its latent state to something more active? As I reflect on this, stewardship can be likened to gardening in some ways:

- *We must choose where to put our efforts. (We wouldn't plant tomatoes in January in Indiana!) We must discern where our resources will do the most good.*
- *Just as healthy plants require nurturing–proper soil preparation, water, fertilizer, weeding, patience–our efforts at outreach and growth also require something of us–some time, some money, a willingness to change both our attitudes and our expectations, a sense of personal responsibility, and some patience.*
- *We shouldn't do it just for the end result. We should enjoy the process. We may not see the desired results on our timetable, but some unexpected product of our efforts may live on far beyond our expectations.*
- *We must work as partners with God.*

Prayer: Gracious God, thank you for all the beautiful growing things in your world. May we be loving and giving caretakers of them. Help us to be partners with you, and bless the efforts we make in your name. Amen.

Day 17: The Seasons of Life
Read Ecclesiastes 3:1-8

September 11 is a painful day for my family. We share with others in grief over the tragedies in New York City, Washington D.C., and in the air over Pennsylvania on that date in 2001. It's also the date on which my mother died in 1996. And it is the date on which we went to the memorial service for a young adult in our family who committed suicide in 2001.

The events of September 11 affected lives all around the world, and we are not alone in having other tragedies connected to that date. It sometimes seems as though tragedies come in clusters. When I pastored in a large urban church, it often seemed to me as though deaths came in threes. One beloved member would die, and it would not be long until the same happened to two more.

Some have called Ecclesiastes a pessimistic book; but the truth, I believe, is that Ecclesiastes reflects the reality of life. There are seasons in our lives just as there are seasons in nature:

* There are wonderful times of joy and celebration.
* There are times of planting and cultivating, when ideas and projects take root and produce results.
* There are times of difficulty when the weeds threaten to take over.
* And there are times when we lose those we love and when our dreams crash.

Matthew 7:24–27 provides a good balance to Ecclesiastes. Christ warns us that storms and trials will come but also reassures us that God will see us through those times: *Everyone then who hears these words of mine and acts on them will be like a wise man who built his house on rock* [v. 24]. Whether those storms are natural or financial, God remains with us.

Prayer: Lord, help us build our lives on the strong foundation of Your love and Your teachings. Stay with us when the storms of life come, and grant us thankful hearts in times of joy and celebration. Amen.

Day 18: Faith in Times of Transition
Read Matthew 7:24–27

Less than a year from the publication of this resource, my wife and I will be living in the metropolitan St. Louis area rather than in Indiana. The business for which my wife worked for many years was acquired by a larger company which then moved her division into a joint venture with yet another company. The the new joint venture will be based in St. Louis, and we need to move there for my wife to continue work with the organization. We do not have school age children at home, and the organization for which I work permits great flexibility.

We consider ourselves more fortunate than many people affected by the acquisition and merger. A relocation is possible for us, and my wife feels very good about the quality of the people and the organization that is emerging from all these changes. The transition, however, will be a very painful one for us in many ways. We love our house in Fort Wayne, Indiana; we love the beautiful yard my wife's efforts have created; and we will have to spend a great deal more on housing in the St. Louis area. We have many very dear friends in our home church in Fort Wayne, and they have been very supportive of us in times of stress in our lives. We have also worked hard to be supportive of them and have, in some instances, been able to make a positive difference in their lives. After we move, I will still have contact with many of these people because I will be coming back to Fort Wayne frequently to work with my professional colleagues. My wife, however, will not be so fortunate.

Our transitions are easier than those people who cannot move to St. Louis and are losing their jobs. We give thanks for the reality that God is with all of us in these transitions. Our challenge is to maintain a foundation on the rock of Christ.

Prayer: Help us, Lord, when we or those we love face difficult transitions in life. Keep us firmly rooted in Your love and good news. Help us remember that You are with us wherever we move or whatever happens. Amen.

Day 19: Transition in the Church
Read 1 Corinthians 1:10–17

"Some of the songs we sing in church these days just don't have any meaning for me. I call it 'throw-up' music because they just throw the words up on this screen that I can't read instead of using a hymnal." The woman was sitting beside me on an airplane and sharing her frustrations with changes in worship at her church. She's not alone in feeling that way!

There are many transitions in society, and there are also transitions in our churches. Many congregations are experiencing one or more of the following:

- A transition from more traditional music with organ accompaniment to more contemporary music with a much wider range of musical instruments.
- A transition from most members having a very high degree of loyalty to the denomination and the local congregation to more members who will change churches if there is a feeling that their needs are not being met by church programs and staff.
- A transition from congregations able to give a great deal of their income to missions outside of the local church walls to congregations finding it difficult to raise enough money to pay their staff and maintain the physical facilities.
- A transition from men wearing suits and women wearing dresses in worship services to both men and women dressing far more informally.

Some of these transitions reflect changes in the larger society. Some are an effort to help the church do more effective outreach to younger people and to those who did not grow up in the church. As we reflect on the changes in our own congregation, we want to be concerned not only about how we personally feel about the changes but about how they affect others.

Prayer: Help us, Lord, in times of transition to recognize that You are still the head and the center of the church. Nurture our faith and strengthen our congregation. Amen.

Day 20: The Eye of the Needle
Read Matthew 19:16–26

I once pastored a large congregation which had a single member whose income was so high that a tithe from him would have been larger than the entire budget of the congregation. He was a very generous person, but he and I agreed that it would not be healthy for too much of the budget to be dependent on his giving. As a result, he made a large pledge to the church's operating budget but did the majority of his charitable giving through the church to a wide range of mission and human need projects that were not part of the budget.

He never used the magnitude of his giving to influence decisions in the congregation, and he was always very gracious when the direction of the church did not coincide with his personal hopes. He was often troubled, however, by the disparity between his financial resources and the great poverty in which so many people lived. A student of the Bible, he talked about his anxiety over Matthew 19:16–26 and wondered if he should consider giving away literally all of his wealth. He did not take that radical a step, but the magnitude of his generosity continually increased.

He once said to me, "I think the reason the New Testament contains so many warnings about the dangers of wealth is that, when you have a great deal of money, you spend so much time and energy worrying about it. You want to use it wisely. You don't want to lose it. You don't want to let down all the people who work for you. And then there is the danger of starting to think that you're better than other people because you have wealth." The "eye of the needle" in biblical times is said by some scholars to have been the intentionally small gate into the city, through which a camel could only enter on its knees. Salvation is not impossible for those of us who are wealthy, but our hearts must be humble. And by the standards of the developing nations of the world, all of us in North America are wealthy.

Prayer: Help us, Lord, to recognize that we have great wealth in comparison to many of the poor in the world. Grant us humble hearts and a willingness to share what You have given us with others. Amen.

Day 21: The Power of E-mail
Read Psalm 42:1–11

I established my first e-mail account about ten years ago. I had difficulty coming up with a name for the account which would be easy for people (including myself) to remember but which would be unique. Variation after variation of my name and my organization's name were already taken. My cat Tia (already revealed in the Day 2 devotion as a powerful influence on me) was sitting on my lap and batting at the keys as I searched for a name. I finally decided to try "DadofTia," which was accepted by the Internet Service Provider. Many years have passed since I sent my first e-mail, and I continue to be impressed by the power of the medium:

- My local church has created an e-mail prayer list. Because of my travel, it wasn't easy for me to participate in the telephone prayer chain, but I can receive the e-mail notifications of need wherever I am and can remember people in prayer.
- I can send communications to people late at night or early in the morning, when I would never think of making a phone call. They can read my greeting at their convenience and reply when they are ready.
- E-mail has helped me develop friendships and links with professional people and committed Christians I've never had the pleasure of meeting in person. We've been able to share information and help each other in sometimes very significant ways.
- I participate in five different "list serves" or e-mail discussion groups through which I receive postings from people who share similar interests and concerns. I can simply "lurk," gaining from the information and discussion without responding, or I can become an active e-mail participant.
- E-mail let me be in contact with my cousin in New York City on September 11, 2001, when I couldn't get any other communication to go through.

Prayer: Thank you, Lord, for the ways in which technology can bring us closer to other people and to You. Help us use the gifts of technology in positive ways rather than becoming addicted to these media. Amen.

Week Four:
What Motivates Us?

Day 22: Making a Difference
Read Proverbs 3:9–10

We feel especially good about our giving when we realize that it is making a difference in the life of the church, in the life of other people, or in our own lives. The president of a primarily African-American, church-related college once said:

I'm excited about the difference my college makes in the lives of young people. I'm excited about the way God has enabled us to take students who barely qualified to start college and then turn them into teachers and social workers and doctors and dentists. And I think there is almost nothing finer that a Christian can do with his or her money than use it to provide scholarships to turn around the lives of these young people. . . .

I'm never apologetic when I ask for money. I'm sharing an opportunity. They have to decide how to respond. . . . I also accept it when they say "no." Overall, I am absolutely convinced that I do as much for the donor as for the recipient. I connect the donor to something greater than himself or herself, and God pulls us all toward that kind of relationship.

When visiting a church I pastored, that president made a direct approach to a somewhat affluent member who was very tight with his money. I thought to myself that the president was simply wasting his time. He wasn't. He got a check for $30,000 from that member. Over a period of time, he persuaded the member to be a trustee of his college and to take a personal interest in the students. He truly changed the life of that church member.

Prayer: Help us, Lord, to find opportunities to make a difference in the lives of others. Open our hearts to the needs around us, and enable us to touch the hearts of others. Amen.

Day 23: Put the Big Rocks in First
2 Corinthians 9:6–8

George Buttrick, a professor at my seminary, warned us that the greatest barrier to effective sermons was the small amount of preparation time from most pastors. He pointed out to us that the administrative tasks of the church, the pastoral care needs of the congregation, and the unending tide of meetings and appointments cause many clergy to keep postponing work on the sermon to later and later in the week. For some, that means doing the majority of the work on Saturday or even early Sunday morning.

He urged us, if we believed good preaching was important, to set aside time each day for that task and to honor that time except in the event of pastoral emergencies. He said, "Organizing your week is just like filling a container with rocks of many different sizes. You need to put the big rocks in first. Then the pebbles and smaller rocks can fit around the big ones. But if you start with the pebbles and small rocks, you'll have no room left for the big ones."

I've heard various time management gurus offer similar advice. We need to determine the tasks that are most important in any given week, protect the time to accomplish them, and then fit the less important tasks around those times.

That is good counsel for the stewardship of time and also for the stewardship of money. When we do our financial planning, we need to determine what the most important things are and set aside the funds for them. Then we can make allocations for lower priority needs and wants. For the Christian, charitable giving becomes one of the "big rocks," as we recognize that all the rocks have come to us from God.

Prayer: Help us, Lord, to be wise in our use of time and material resources. Guide us in taking care of the big rocks first and then the smaller ones. Amen.

Day 24: Growth in Giving
Read Proverbs 3:9–10

The traditional standard of giving within the church has been the tithe, or 10% of one's income. My personal belief is that the tithe is a good biblical standard for us but that we need to view everything we have as having come from God. There are people in very difficult circumstances for whom a tithe at the present time is impossible, and there are people who have been so richly blessed that a tithe is not a sufficient level of giving.

Most Christians give considerably less than a tithe, and the jump to a full tithe can feel too great for many. The approach which has proven effective for a great many people is to calculate the percentage of income currently being given and then to raise that percentage between 1% and 4% each year until a full tithe has been achieved. The household with a $65,000 income and a current giving level of $2,600, or 4%, might decide to move to 6% next year, then to 8%, and then to 10% in the third year. For those who have not been giving on a regular basis, an initial move to a few dollars each week may be a major step forward. Others may find, on prayerful reflection, that they will feel best if they immediately move to a tithe. Some feel called to give more than a tithe. The final decision must be made prayerfully by each one of us. This chart may be of help.

Growth in Giving as % of Annual Income

Income	3%	4%	5%	6%	7%	8%	9%	10%
100,000	3000	4000	5000	6000	7000	8000	9000	10,000
75,000	2250	3000	3750	4500	5250	6000	6750	7500
65,000	1950	2600	3250	3900	4550	5200	5850	6500
55,000	1650	2200	2750	3300	3850	4400	4950	5500
45,000	1350	1800	2250	2700	3150	3600	4050	4500
35,000	1050	1400	1750	2100	2450	2800	3150	3500
25,000	750	1000	1250	1500	1750	2000	2250	2500
20,000	600	800	1000	1200	1400	1600	1800	2000
15,000	450	600	750	900	1050	1200	1350	1500

Prayer: Help us, Lord, to reflect carefully on our level of giving. Open our hearts to the reality that all we have comes from You and that You continually seek to bless us. Amen.

Day 25: Money to Buy a House
Read Matthew 18:1–5

Several years ago, I had the good fortune to spend six months living as the guest of a family with three young children. Near the end of my time in their household, I was making plans to buy a home and had talked about wanting to make as large a down payment as possible. Jenna, who was four years old at the time, came to me one evening with her hands full of pennies, nickels, quarters, a few crumpled one dollar bills, and a fairly substantial amount of "play money." She gave it to me and said that she hoped I could use that to buy my house. In love, she had offered me all the money that she had!

Jenna wasn't worried about giving me everything. She knew that her parents would continue to provide for her needs. She was, however, ready to give up the special purchases for which she had been saving money.

In the Gospel of Luke [21:1–4], a widow willingly offers everything to our Lord. She recognized God as the source of what she had. Such generosity isn't possible in North American society. We have mortgage payments, health insurance payments, car payments, medical bills, utility bills, and all kinds of other expenses. God does not intend for us to do without the things that we need and in fact makes many luxuries available to us. Jenna and the widow teach us, however, that we can too easily be dependent on our wealth and that God will provide for us no matter what happens. The confusion between *needs* and *wants* in our society keeps most of us from the kind of generosity which should be possible.

Our Lord wants good things for us, and most of us have been richly blessed. We cannot give away all that we have, but we can recognize that all that we have comes from You.

Prayer: Help us, Lord, to develop hearts which are more generous. Help us consider how we might better share our blessings with the church and with those in need. Amen.

Day 26: Not Dressed For Success
Matthew 16:24–25

At a workshop I conducted on congregational outreach to young adults, a delightful woman in her seventies shared this story with me: *There is a young adult who's started coming to our church who just made me crazy for months. He would always come shuffling into church late and would sit down in my pew. I know he has a job programming computers or something like that, but he dresses like a bum. His clothes look like he slept in them, and I don't think he washes his hair more than once a week.*

One Sunday, just after he sat down in the pew, the pastor made an announcement about a woman in our congregation who was in danger of losing her house because of all the medical bills she had accumulated while her husband was hospitalized. The pastor told us that we would be taking a special offering to help her.

I saw this young man take out his checkbook. I'll admit this wasn't very charitable of me, but I found myself thinking that he would probably give $10 or $20 to this woman but nothing more. Well, I found myself leaning over, like I was reaching for a hymnal, so that I could see what was in his checkbook.

I was just amazed. I saw him record the check in his register. He had a bank balance of $860, and he had written a check for $825 to help this woman. He was leaving himself $35 in the bank for whatever he had to purchase before he received more income. Now he might have had some money in savings or a mutual fund or something, but I was deeply moved.

After the service, I started a conversation with him. He said to me, "I feel so sorry for that woman who risked everything for her husband. I think about all the money that I wasted in the last month and how much more I could have given if I had been more careful. I hope God takes care of her." And God certainly blessed me with a new vision of the character of this young man.

Prayer: Help us, Lord, not to judge others on the basis of external appearances or wealth. Teach us to see your love and your presence reflected in the lives of others. Amen.

Day 27: Measuring Our Worth
Read Luke 12:22–31

A wonderful couple, who are very dear friends of mine, shared with me their frustration over their lives. They were approaching retirement and realized that they did not have the kind of financial resources many of their friends did.

They had two children of their own, shared their home with several foster children, and adopted three children from another country. They continually dealt with the cost of clothing, school, and medical expenses. Because there were so many demands at home, the wife only worked part-time most of her life and missed out on the upward mobility that could have been hers in her chosen profession.

As they visited with me, they shared a feeling of failure for not having accumulated more during their lives. They felt like they should have been smarter in their investments, more careful with their money, and more conscious of the need to advance in their respective careers.

But I saw them as a very wealthy couple. They were good parents to their own children, and they changed the lives of the foster children and the children they adopted. They were extremely active in the church and generous in their contributions to worthy causes. Their wealth could not be measured in financial terms, but it was very real, and few people have so much. Of course I shared my observations with them.

Our society encourages us to measure ourselves and others by social status, income, and material possessions. The message of Scripture is very different. Christ's love extends to us regardless of our material resources. Scripture warns us of the dangers of wealth and tells us that there are blessings for the poor. The standards of society should not be our standards.

Prayer: Lord, deliver us from the temptation to measure the worth of ourselves and of others by social status, income, or possessions. Fill our hearts with thanksgiving, and direct our lives in Your service. Amen.

Day 28: A Full Calendar
Read Deuteronomy 8:10 and 2 Corinthians 9:8

As I complete this devotional booklet, my calendar for the week ahead is filled with commitments involving food. I have a total of six breakfast or lunch meetings planned with coworkers who are also friends, and I have three evenings sharing dinner with friends. My wife and I are both traveling part of the week, but we will get to share some meals together.

I greatly enjoy good food and exercise, which is a positive combination since the regular exercise makes it possible for me to enjoy the food, including dessert, without guilt. I also find the sharing of meals with friends and family a very meaningful experience. In the breaking of bread together, I find that we open our hearts to each other and to Christ's presence in a different kind of way.

When I find myself having difficulty working with a person or involved in a strong difference of opinion with someone, I have learned that sharing a meal together can be an excellent way to open up communication.

The sharing of Holy Communion (or the Eucharist–the terminology depends on your tradition) in church opens our hearts to one another and brings us into direct connection with our risen Lord. God, who has given us all the food that we enjoy as well as the other blessings of our lives, gave us the greatest gift in Christ. All our giving and all our living should be an expression of our thanks for God's enormous generosity.

Prayer: Help us, Lord, to open our hearts and our minds to Your presence in one another and in the life of the church. Fill our hearts with thanksgiving, and help our gratitude overflow to others. Amen.